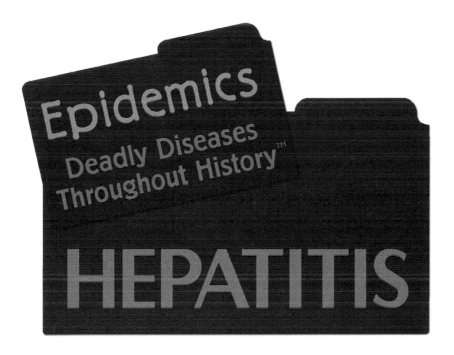

AILEEN GALLAGHER

Epidemics

Deadly Diseases
Throughout History™

HEPATITIS

The Rosen Publishing Group, Inc.
New York

For Rebekah Stackpole, generous with both
knowledge and laughter

Published in 2005 by The Rosen Publishing Group, Inc.
29 East 21st Street, New York, NY 10010

Library of Congress Cataloging-in-Publication Data

Gallagher, Aileen.
Hepatitis/by Aileen Gallagher.—1st ed.
    p. cm.—Epidemics)
Includes index.
ISBN 1-4042-0255-2 (library binding)
1. Hepatitis—Juvenile literature. 2. Hepatitis—History—
Juvenile literature.
I. Title. II. Series.
RC848.H42G34 2005
616.3'623—dc22

                                            2004016703

Manufactured in the United States of America

On the cover: A photomicrograph of the Lassa virus, which
causes hepatitis.

CONTENTS

In October 2002, New Jersey assemblyman Louis Greenwald (center) received a hepatitis B vaccine injection at a press conference. New Jersey was the first state in the United States to pass legislation requiring all high school students to be vaccinated against hepatitis B before 2003.

INTRODUCTION

O n October 5, 2003, John Spratt and his teenage daughter shared a plate of chicken fajitas at a chain restaurant called Chi-Chi's near Pittsburgh, Pennsylvania. In the weeks after their dinner, Spratt felt like he had a case of the flu that wouldn't go away.

When his symptoms worsened a third time and Spratt could no longer keep any food or water down, his doctor sent him to the hospital to be treated for dehydration. "And then he unexpectedly went into liver failure," Spratt's brother, Joseph, told the *Pittsburgh Post-Gazette*. Spratt was admitted to the hospital on November 5. His doctors wanted to give him an immediate liver transplant, but Spratt never recovered long enough to undergo the surgery.

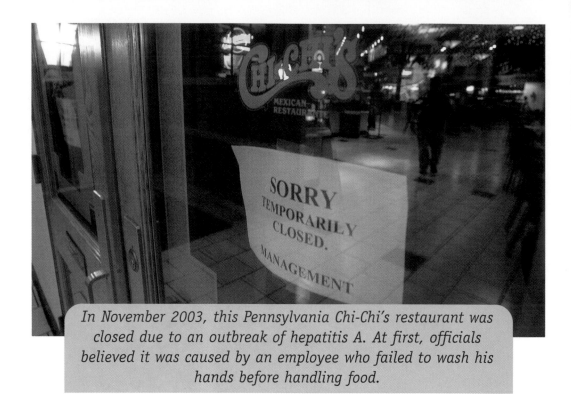

In November 2003, this Pennsylvania Chi-Chi's restaurant was closed due to an outbreak of hepatitis A. At first, officials believed it was caused by an employee who failed to wash his hands before handling food.

He died on November 14, 2003, a victim of one of the largest hepatitis A outbreaks in the country.

Spratt was one of three victims who died of hepatitis A after contracting the disease from the Pittsburgh-area restaurant. The Pennsylvania Department of Health first learned about the outbreak in early November. It opened clinics and asked everyone who had eaten at the restaurant to be screened, or tested, for hepatitis A. Out of the 10,000 people who were screened in March 2004, 660 of them tested positive for hepatitis A, according to the Associated Press. Those who did not test positive were given an injection of immune globulin, a drug that kept them from getting the disease.

Workers in a Mexican processing plant sort green onions before they are put through a disinfectant bath and readied for export. A hepatitis outbreak linked to imported green onions from Mexico in 2003 forced the Mexican government to implement a new health inspection system.

The doctors at the health department could not determine why people were getting so sick. People with poor hygiene often spread hepatitis A when they do not wash their hands after using the bathroom. But considering that so many people were sick, and many of the people had eaten at Chi-Chi's on different days, doctors suspected that the food itself was contaminated with hepatitis A, possibly before it got to Chi-Chi's. The disease was eventually traced to tainted green onions that Chi-Chi's bought from Mexico and put in its food. Chi-Chi's was not the only chain to have ordered the shipment of tainted onions. On November 22, 2003, the Associated Press reported that the onions could have been contaminated in several ways, possibly from a sewage leak in a farmer's field or due to an unwashed truck that hauled the produce.

Before the outbreak, it is likely that none of the people in Pittsburgh had ever thought much about hepatitis. Hepatitis A, a disease spread mostly by people with poor hygiene, is rare in developed countries like the United States. However, as the Chi-Chi's outbreak showed, hepatitis A can affect anyone, as it did John Spratt.

Hepatitis A shares its name with other varieties of the same disease, such as hepatitis B and C. All types of hepatitis eventually attack the liver. Hepatitis is often treatable, though in some cases it can end in death. Most important, hepatitis is a disease that can often be avoided by taking certain precautions, such as hand-washing and practicing safe, protected sex. Knowing about hepatitis, and how to prevent it, is the best way of avoiding the disease and stopping an epidemic in its tracks.

1

SPREADING THE VIRUS

There are at least five forms of hepatitis known to scientists and all of them cause inflammation, or swelling, of the liver. Doctors call the different forms hepatitis A, B, C, D, and E. Each form of the disease is contracted by humans in different ways and often exhibits unique symptoms. The Centers for Disease Control and Prevention (CDC), a U.S. government agency that studies and tries to prevent diseases, collects information about all forms of hepatitis to educate the public.

People get hepatitis A from coming into contact with the feces of an infected person. Most often, people who do not wash their hands after using the bathroom spread hepatitis A. For example, someone named John has hepatitis A.

Raw sewage pours onto Rosarito Beach in Baja California, Mexico, in August 1993. Increased industrialization in the region has led to increased pollution and to rising rates of salmonella, shigella, cholera, malaria, and hepatitis among local populations and tourists. The United States–Mexico Border Health Commission continues to monitor disease rates in this area.

John works in a restaurant and is not always careful about washing his hands after he goes to the bathroom. At the restaurant, John often touches food that is not thoroughly cooked. (Cooking food usually kills the virus.) A patron orders a salad that is prepared by John and then eats food that John has contaminated.

Hepatitis A is rare in the United States and other wealthy nations because it is easier for people to practice good hygiene. Sewage is treated and contained, and not allowed to run into streets or fields where it could encounter fruits and vegetables. Garbage with dirty diapers or contaminated food is not kept in places where people live. Hot running water makes keeping clean easier, too.

What makes spreading hepatitis A easy is that people often don't know they are infected. John the restaurant worker probably has no idea that he is infected with the disease. People with hepatitis A can feel tired or nauseated, have fevers, lose their appetites, or have stomachaches. In some cases, patients will have jaundice, or a yellow tinge to their skin and eyes. They may also expel urine that seems darker than normal. In many cases, hepatitis A tends to incubate for about thirty days before symptoms appear. After the incubation period, an infected person experiences nausea, vomiting, abdominal pain, and a decreased appetite. Jaundice, itching, and darkened urine appear about two weeks later, as initial symptoms decrease.

For the most part, hepatitis A feels a lot like the flu. The symptoms last less than two months for most people and the infection is gone. Since hepatitis A can be diagnosed only with a blood test, many people are infected with the virus without knowing it.

Hepatitis has an incubation period in the body of about thirty days. This means when a person is infected, it takes about thirty days for symptoms to appear. However, the CDC says thirty days is not an absolute number. To be certain that one is without disease, the incubation range is fifteen to fifty days. For example, by mid-January 2004, the Pennsylvania Health Department reported that there were no new cases of hepatitis A related to the Chi-Chi's outbreak. Fifty days had passed since the first case of hepatitis A, and doctors felt that the incubation period was over.

There are two vaccines for hepatitis A. Because the disease is so rare in the United States, the vaccine is given only to someone at risk of contracting the disease. For instance, if someone were going to visit a country with poor sanitation and hygiene, he or she would likely get the vaccine before his or her trip. (According to the CDC, Mexico, Bolivia, Paraguay, much of the Middle East, and nearly all of Africa have high rates of hepatitis A.) However, if a person is exposed to hepatitis A, he or she can be injected with immune globulin to prevent infection. In order for the immune globulin to work, the person must be injected with it within two weeks of his or her exposure to the virus.

Only in very few cases does hepatitis A continue to cause problems after the initial acute infection. Medically, "acute" means "having a rapid onset and following a short but severe course." The hepatitis A virus does not typically do long-term damage to the liver.

Hepatitis B

The CDC estimates that 78,000 people in the United States contracted hepatitis B in 2001. About 5,000 people died from hepatitis B that year. Today, about 1.25 million Americans have the virus.

Hepatitis B is spread by coming into contact with the blood or body fluids of an infected person. Sharing intravenous needles and having unprotected sex with infected people are the most common ways of contracting the virus, which is easier to contract than HIV. Also, mothers infected with hepatitis B can pass the virus to their babies during the birthing process. Hepatitis B is not spread through casual contact, such as shaking hands with or hugging an infected person.

As with other forms of the virus, it is possible to have hepatitis B and not know it. Only a blood test can confirm if someone has the virus. The symptoms for hepatitis A and B can be similar, too. Infected people can feel flulike symptoms, such as joint pain or fever. Hepatitis B can also make people extremely tired. At times, people with hepatitis B are unable to get up and go to school or work for weeks or even months.

There is a vaccine for hepatitis B, which must be given in three doses. These doses are injected months apart, depending on the age of the patient.

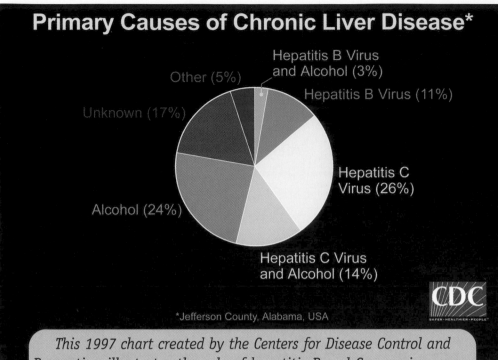

Primary Causes of Chronic Liver Disease*

Hepatitis B Virus and Alcohol (3%)

Other (5%)

Hepatitis B Virus (11%)

Unknown (17%)

Hepatitis C Virus (26%)

Alcohol (24%)

Hepatitis C Virus and Alcohol (14%)

CDC

*Jefferson County, Alabama, USA

This 1997 chart created by the Centers for Disease Control and Prevention illustrates the role of hepatitis B and C as major causes of liver disease in Jefferson County, Alabama. Poorer counties like Jefferson tend to have higher concentrations of disease due to less access to medical care and higher rates of substance abuse.

The vaccine keeps the body from being infected with hepatitis B for a person's entire life. Since hepatitis B can also cause liver cancer, the vaccine is also the first to possibly prevent cancer.

About 90 to 95 percent of people infected with hepatitis B recover fully and are immune to the virus for the rest of their lives. The remaining 5 to 10 percent become carriers of the disease, at risk for developing chronic infections. Older hepatitis B patients sometimes develop chronic liver diseases, such as cirrhosis.

Hepatitis C

Hepatitis C can only be spread through direct contact with infected blood. Some people get hepatitis C from sharing intravenous needles. Others have the virus because they received blood or organs from an infected person. Although hepatitis C can be spread through unprotected sexual contact, contracting the disease in this way is rare. The disease cannot be spread by sharing eating utensils or drinks with, hugging, or being sneezed or coughed upon by an infected person. People with hepatitis C are at little risk of infecting those with whom they live, work, or go to school.

Hepatitis C sometimes causes flulike symptoms similar to those of hepatitis A and B, but it can also be asymptomatic, which means that it shows no symptoms at all. However, chronic hepatitis C can do more significant liver damage than other types of hepatitis can. Of every 100 people who have hepatitis C, seventy-five to eighty-five of them may develop long-term, or chronic, infections, and seventy may develop chronic liver disease. Another fifteen of those 100 people infected could, over twenty to thirty years, develop cirrhosis of the liver. Because hepatitis C is so damaging to the liver, people with the disease are often candidates for liver transplants.

In 2001, Pennsylvania governor Mark Schweiker (right) *signed a law giving firefighters, paramedics, and police officers the right to workers' compensation if they contract hepatitis C on the job.*

There are three different types of blood tests to determine if one is infected with hepatitis C. The first test detects if your body is producing antibodies to fight hepatitis C. The second test finds out if the virus is present in your blood. The third test reveals how much of the virus is present in your blood. Since hepatitis C does not show up in blood tests until one or two weeks after infection, and symptoms may take months to appear (if they appear at all), doctors often use a combination of the three blood tests to confirm a hepatitis C diagnosis. Detecting hepatitis C is difficult, and though the virus can appear in the body in just days, it can show up at any time during an eight-week period. The speed at which it appears depends upon the the amount of virus to which the person was exposed.

People with hepatitis C can be treated with interferon therapy. These drugs help jump-start a patient's immune system to help it fight the virus more quickly. There is no cure for hepatitis C, but interferon therapy can slow the damage the virus causes.

Hepatitis D and Hepatitis E

People with hepatitis D (also called the delta virus) cannot have it without also having hepatitis B. Hepatitis D is an "incomplete" virus. In order to contract hepatitis D, a person needs to already be infected with the hepatitis B virus. Having hepatitis B does not automatically mean someone will also get hepatitis D. The hepatitis D symptoms are similar to those of hepatitis B, though hepatitis D can cause more severe liver damage.

Hepatitis E is similar to hepatitis A in that it is mainly transmitted by drinking water contaminated by diseased fecal matter. Unlike hepatitis A, it is rare

The word "virus" comes from the Latin word *virus*, which means poison. A virus is a microorganism made of either deoxyribonucleic acid (DNA) or ribonucleic acid (RNA), the materials that make up genes.

A virus is not alive and depends on other cells to spread throughout the body in a form called a virion. A virion is a virus particle made up of a protein shell covering a DNA or RNA core. When a virion enters the body, it is attracted to specific cells. The hepatitis virus is drawn to liver cells. A virion tricks a part of the healthy cell called the receptor into thinking they should fuse together. When the virion joins the healthy cell, the protein shell breaks down and the genetic material in the virion takes over the organelles of the healthy cell. The RNA or DNA instructs the cell to replicate, or copy, itself. New virions go on to find other healthy cells to take over. Since the liver keeps making new healthy cells, there's a never-ending supply for the virions.

Eventually, so many healthy cells become infected with the virus that a person feels sick. A healthy liver regenerates all its cells about every two years. With hepatitis C, infected cells die faster and force the liver to make new ones at an increased rate. This sometimes causes cirrhosis, or scarring of the liver.

for hepatitis E to be passed from person to person by food or touch. Nearly all reported cases of hepatitis E in the United States occur in people exposed to the virus in countries with poor sanitary conditions.

Hepatitis E is less likely to cause infection that hepatitis A. Although the virus has a low fatality rate of 1 percent, women, especially pregnant women, are at a much greater risk of dying from hepatitis E.

Remember that unprotected sex with multiple partners and sharing drug needles can spread hepatitis B. Sharing needles can also spread hepatitis C. These are the same risky behaviors that also spread the human immunodeficiency virus, or HIV. HIV is the virus that causes AIDS, or acquired immunodeficiency syndrome. According to the CDC, about one-quarter of those infected with HIV also have hepatitis C. Because HIV weakens the immune system, hepatitis acts faster in those with HIV. Those who are co-infected with hepatitis C and HIV should be vaccinated against hepatitis A and B.

Social Stigma

Since few people know a lot about hepatitis, the disease carries with it a certain reputation. What people do know about hepatitis is that certain types of it can be transferred sexually or by sharing needles for intravenous drug use. Others who are ignorant of the disease but know that hepatitis affects the liver confuse it with the symptoms of cirrhosis (which can be one of the effects of hepatitis, but which is also caused by long-term alcoholism).

People with hepatitis often feel ashamed of the disease because of how they contracted it. Those who got hepatitis C from a tainted blood transfusion often have to reassure their friends and loved ones that they did not get the disease from having unprotected sex or using drugs. People might treat someone differently after learning that he or she has the disease. Besides dealing with the physical aspects of hepatitis, the chronic nature of some types of hepatitis can be emotionally difficult. As a result, some hepatitis patients experience depression related to the disease.

2

A SILENT EPIDEMIC

When people think of an epidemic, they probably think of AIDS or the black plague. Those are traditional epidemics, diseases that spread rapidly and affect many individuals in a specific location at the same time. Hepatitis, because it can be transmitted in different ways and often does not kill people, is a disease not often considered an epidemic.

It is easy to assume that like AIDS, hepatitis spreads rapidly and is considered an outbreak. An outbreak of hepatitis A, such as the one in Pittsburgh, hits many people at once. But in most instances, these people recover. It is unlikely that a hepatitis A outbreak will result in the deaths of thousands of people, like the plague outbreak did. Hepatitis B is, for most people, a one-time infection. Although the disease can become chronic, a good portion of those who are infected with hepatitis B will recover. In addition, vaccinations against hepatitis A and B keep the disease from spreading in the first place.

Dr. C. Everett Koop, U.S. surgeon general from 1982 to 1989, served under presidents Ronald Reagan and George H. W. Bush. Since his retirement, Dr. Koop has continued to give presentations about preventing diseases such as hepatitis and AIDS.

Hepatitis C, though, has the characteristics of an epidemic. Former U.S. surgeon general C. Everett Koop thinks hepatitis C is "one of the most significant preventable and treatable public health problems facing our nation today." According to the C. Everett Koop Institute in New Hampshire, more than 4 million people in the United States, and as many as 200 million people in the world, are infected with hepatitis C. To put these numbers in perspective, hepatitis C infects three times as many people as AIDS. One-third of all liver transplants performed in America are caused by hepatitis C.

Around the world, 75 percent of all liver disease is related to hepatitis C.

Research gathered by the Koop Institute shows that, in the United States, the African American community has the highest rate of infection of hepatitis C, followed by Native Americans, Hispanics, and whites. Besides ethnic groups, certain other populations are more likely to get hepatitis C than others. Low-income populations get infected more than middle- or upper-class groups. People in prison are also at a higher risk of infection of hepatitis C. Some prisons have a hepatitis C infection rate of more than 80 percent.

The body's immune system is better at overcoming hepatitis A and B than hepatitis C. The immune system will fight hepatitis for years and years but never beat the disease. About 80 to 90 percent of hepatitis C infections eventually lead to chronic liver disease. Because the immune system tries too hard to fight the virus, people with hepatitis C often feel as though they have the flu. Flulike symptoms will come and go over the years, so those who have hepatitis C often don't even know they are sick. Not only does this make it easier for carriers to spread the virus, but it also makes it harder for them to be treated. Since people don't know they are sick, they won't seek the medical help that could prevent extensive liver damage. This is why some doctors refer to hepatitis C as "the silent epidemic."

According to Dr. Koop, "We stand at the precipice of a grave threat to our public health. It affects people from all walks of life, in every state, in every country. And unless we do something about it soon, it will kill more people than AIDS." The Koop Institute believes there are several reasons hepatitis C is so untreated and misunderstood.

- The public knows so little about hepatitis C that it is not concerned about the disease. Few people get tested for hepatitis C like they get tested for AIDS.

- Because hepatitis C was only discovered in 1989, many doctors know little about it. They do not know the symptoms to look for in patients, so they cannot order the correct tests or treatment.

- Because hepatitis C can take fifteen or even twenty years to show the most severe symptoms, people infected with the virus do not get the treatment they need and can spread the disease without knowing it. Very often they won't experience any symptoms.

- Medical research often takes years to yield results, so some of the information doctors are learning from is recent.

- Although hepatitis C is a virus that mutates, or changes, frequently, blood tests can now reveal if the virus is present in the body. Although it is easy to determine whether of not a person has hepatitis C, many people never think to get tested because they experience no symptoms.

- Because it takes such a tiny amount of blood to spread the virus, almost 40 percent of people known to be infected with hepatitis C have no idea how they got the disease. Also, because people don't know they could be infected, they do not get tested and can unknowingly spread the disease.

- Poorer, less developed countries do not spread information about hepatitis C that could help people get treated or learn ways to prevent infection.

As doctors and scientists learn more about hepatitis C and pass that information on to the public, education has helped stem infection rates. Research gathered by the Koop Institute shows that in the 1980s, about 180,000 people a year contracted hepatitis C. In 1995, only about 28,000 new cases were reported. The Koop Institute believes that more than 200 million people around the world, or about 3.3 percent of the world's population, are infected with some form of hepatitis.

3

AN ANCIENT EPIDEMIC

Although it is impossible to know exactly when hepatitis first appeared in humans, some of its symptoms have existed for centuries. According to the medical journal *Clinical Microbiology Review*, epidemic jaundice (a symptom of hepatitis) appeared in ancient Greece and Rome. An epidemic is a widespread outbreak of infectious disease during which many people are infected at the same time. The first modern record of epidemic jaundice is from an outbreak on the Mediterranean island of Minorca in 1745. While scientists do not know for sure if this jaundice indicated a hepatitis outbreak, there was certainly a contagious disease on Minorca that affected the liver.

According to *Clinical Microbiology*, a scientist named H. C. Brown was studying jaundice

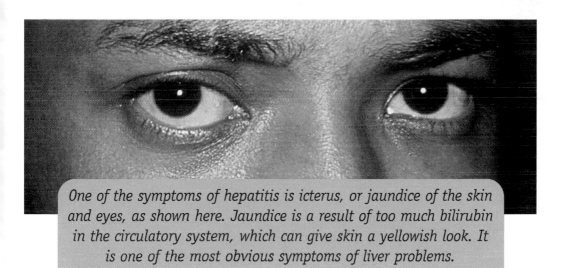

One of the symptoms of hepatitis is icterus, or jaundice of the skin and eyes, as shown here. Jaundice is a result of too much bilirubin in the circulatory system, which can give skin a yellowish look. It is one of the most obvious symptoms of liver problems.

outbreaks in England in 1931. He determined that the jaundice was caused by an "ultra-microscopic virus which is pathogenic only to man," meaning the virus appeared only in humans, not animals. Brown himself developed symptoms less than five weeks after handling samples from an outbreak in Yorkshire. This time span between infection and showing symptoms was the first hint doctors had about the actual incubation period of hepatitis.

Although doctors did not yet have a name for hepatitis, they learned a lot about the virus simply from studying outbreaks. By the early 1900s, doctors had learned that hepatitis passed from person to person through food and possibly water. Some scientists mistakenly thought that the virus passed through sneezing and coughing, like the common cold. Scientists at Yale University in Connecticut studied hepatitis during World War II (1939–1945).

2000 BC
First recorded references to jaundice and other hepatitis symptoms.

1947
F. O. MacCallum identifies and names hepatitis A, spread by food and water, and hepatitis B, spread by blood.

1963
Baruch S. Blumberg and Harvey Alter discover the Aa antigen (later called HBsAg), later linked to hepatitis.

1973–1974
Stephen Feinstone and Maurice Hilleman identify and describe the hepatitis A virus.

1980–1981
A hepatitis B vaccine is developed by Hilleman and approved for public use.

1983
Mikhail Balayan identifies hepatitis E.

Their test subjects were conscientious objectors, or men who refused to fight in the war on moral or religious grounds. From the tests, doctors learned more about the virus's incubation period and how it spread.

1968
Kazuo Okochi's experiments confirm that hepatitis is a virus and hepatitis B is spread through blood.

1971
Saul Krugman accidentally discovers that heating blood infected with hepatitis B could kill the virus.

1972
The United States requires all donated blood to be tested for hepatitis B.

1990
Tests are developed to find hepatitis C in blood.

1996
Hilleman develops a hepatitis A vaccine. The first interferon treatment for hepatitis C is developed.

2004
The Associated Press reports that the hepatitis B virus is on the rise among American adults.

Early Research

The National Academy of Sciences describes the early hepatitis research this way. In 1947, a British doctor named F. O. MacCallum was researching yellow fever. Yellow fever, a deadly disease spread by mosquitoes, was killing British soldiers in Africa and South America. While working on a vaccine for yellow fever, Dr. MacCallum discovered that several of the soldiers who were injected with a vaccine developed hepatitis a few months later. Part of the vaccine was made from human serum, the clear, yellowish fluid left over when blood is separated into its solid and liquid parts. The yellow fever vaccine had bits of other people's blood in it. Dr. MacCallum also learned of other cases of hepatitis that came from unsterilized needles and surgical instruments used in hospitals. Hepatitis, he found, could also be spread by blood. Dr. MacCallum's research led him to call the two separate viruses hepatitis A and B.

After Dr. MacCallum's discovery, hepatitis research slowed. Scientists could not isolate the different aspects of hepatitis A and B. As in Dr. MacCallum's case, the next breakthrough in hepatitis would come from a scientist who wasn't even studying the disease.

Dr. Baruch S. Blumberg was interested in why some people were more susceptible to diseases than others. In the early 1950s, he was conducting research in Suriname (a country in South America) and learned that some Surinamese were more prone to contracting a disease called elephantiasis, which is spread by parasites. Because some villagers got elephantiasis and others did not, Dr. Blumberg had an idea that some Surinamese had a genetic makeup that was resistant to the disease. The scientific instruments Dr. Blumberg needed to prove his thesis had not yet been invented. Instead, Dr. Blumberg began to look at differences in the blood proteins present in all humans. These differences, called polymorphisms, were thought to be the genetic differences that helped some people survive illness while others died. Dr. Blumberg traveled all over the world collecting blood samples from different ethnic groups. He also wanted to obtain blood samples from people who had received several blood transfusions to learn what happened when one person's blood was mixed with that of another.

Working with another scientist named Harvey Alter from the National Institutes of Health blood bank, Dr. Blumberg found in 1963 that a blood sample of an Australian aborigine clotted with the blood sample of a hemophiliac in New York. Hemophiliacs have blood that won't clot and often require blood transfusions. The part of the blood that reacted, the antigen, is rarely found in healthy people's blood. Instead, the doctors often found the antigen in people who received many blood transfusions. They named the antigen Aa, or Australian antigen. The antigen is now called HBsAg.

After his help in discovering the Australian antigen in 1963, Dr. Harvey Alter continued his research into the causes of hepatitis and was awarded the Albert Lasker Medical Research Award in 2000 for his achievements.

Scientists began looking for HBsAg in people with leukemia to determine if the antigen was one of the causes of the disease. They also tested people with Down syndrome, who are susceptible to leukemia. In 1966, Blumberg, W. Thomas London, and Alton Sutnik discovered that a twelve-year-old boy acquired HBsAg months after he had tested negative for the antigen. During that time, the boy was also diagnosed with hepatitis. It seemed that HBsAg was linked to hepatitis. The link made even more sense after Dr. Blumberg's lab technician came down with hepatitis. She tested her own blood for HBsAg, and there it was. The technician became one of the first people diagnosed with hepatitis through the HBsAg test.

While scientists all over the world were researching the HBsAg link to hepatitis B, Dr. Alfred Prince at the New York Blood Center took blood samples from several patients who had received multiple transfusions. In 1968, one of Dr. Prince's patients began showing symptoms of hepatitis. In the early samples of the man's blood, there was no HBsAg. After the patient started feeling ill, however, blood tests revealed the presence of HBsAg.

At the University of Tokyo in Japan, also in 1968, a scientist named Kazuo Okochi found that blood that tested positive for HBsAg was much more likely to transmit hepatitis to patients than blood that tested negative. In 1970, doctors at Middlesex Hospital in London saw virus particles in the blood of people with HBsAg. They also saw the virus in liver cells of patients with hepatitis. These discoveries confirmed much of what scientists had been thinking for years. Hepatitis was a virus, and, in the case of hepatitis B, it was passed through the blood.

The scientific method is how scientists solve problems. Without using the scientific method, research would be random. By using the method, all scientists conduct research in the same organized fashion.

Observation: Scientists ask questions about their surroundings. They see the sun rising and setting, water running downhill, or bread getting moldy. After observing, a scientist thinks of a question that could have a precise answer. A scientist could ask, "Why does some bread develop mold?" because that question is answerable.

Hypothesis: After coming up with a question, a scientist then thinks of an answer to that question. This answer, which may not be accurate, is called a hypothesis. In the hypothesis, the scientist thinks of a logical answer to his or her question.

Make predictions: Using the hypothesis, a scientist makes predictions about how it answers his or her questions. For example, if bread left out in a humid room grows mold, the scientist might predict that bread in airtight containers will not spoil as fast. Therefore, bread does not react well to moisture.

Test: Next, the scientist tests his or her predictions. In these experiments, the scientist might disprove his or her hypothesis. What he or she learns from the experiments will change the hypothesis.

Repeat: Scientists continue to experiment until their hypothesis fits the test's results.

Now that doctors knew where hepatitis B came from, they began working on a vaccination to prevent the disease from spreading. In 1971, Saul Krugman, an infectious disease specialist at New York University, made an accidental discovery. Krugman learned that samples of hepatitis B–contaminated blood that had been heated to kill viruses gave some protection against the spread of the disease. Dr. Blumberg, then at Fox Chase Cancer Center in Philadelphia, Pennsylvania, thought that a vaccine could be made from particles of HBsAg.

Dr. Blumberg's idea was unique. Previously, vaccines had largely been made from weakened strains of a virus. In a few cases, they were made from similar viruses. Also, vaccines could be made from whole viruses or bacteria that were killed using heat or cold to prevent infection.

What Dr. Blumberg proposed was using only little pieces, or subunits, of a virus. Maurice Hilleman at the Merck Institute for Science Education thought Dr. Blumberg had the right idea. With permission from Fox Chase, Hilleman started work on using subunits to make a vaccine in 1971. It was not until 1980 that the Merck team created a vaccine that was 90 percent effective against hepatitis B and, most important, had no adverse side effects. The vaccine was made available to the public in 1981.

The only problem with the vaccine was that its production required large amounts of hepatitis B–infected blood. In 1977, William Rutter at the University of California, San Francisco, solved the problem. Rutter learned how to make the virus automatically replicate itself in a process called recombinant technology. Not only could large batches of the vaccine be produced, but there would be no danger of the vaccine containing blood tainted from other diseases. Today, more and more children are being vaccinated against the disease and fewer people are being infected with hepatitis B.

Dr. Maurice Hilleman is seen in this 2003 image at the Walter Reed Research Institute, where he was studying the flu virus. Hilleman was instrumental in identifying and describing the hepatitis A virus in the early 1970s.

The research into hepatitis B encouraged other scientists to learn more about the other

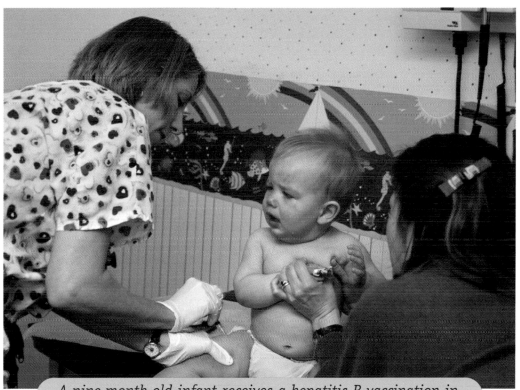

A nine-month-old infant receives a hepatitis B vaccination in 2000. The CDC recommends hepatitis B vaccinations for young children, especially those in high-risk populations or whose mothers have the disease.

forms of hepatitis. In 1973, scientists at the National Institutes of Health used an electron microscope to see the hepatitis A virus in human stools for the first time. Hilleman used his work from hepatitis B to find a vaccine for hepatitis A. In 1996, Hilleman and his colleague Stephen Feinstone developed a vaccine made from a modified version of the hepatitis A virus. Tests to determine the presence of hepatitis C in the blood were not developed until 1990. However, since

A physician examines a man with smallpox scars in Africa during a World Health Organization smallpox eradication campaign.

Since the time of ancient Egypt, smallpox was an epidemic for which there was no cure. People who caught the disease would first develop a high fever and then a rash of small, pus-filled blisters. Smallpox killed about 30 percent of those infected and was spread through coughing and sneezing, like the common cold.

In 1796, Edward Jenner noticed that women who milked cows infected with cowpox (a similar disease affecting only cows) got some blisters but never succumbed to smallpox. Even when everyone in their village got the disease, the milkmaids never got sick. Jenner thought that having cowpox provided some kind of protection against smallpox. His research led to the development of the very first smallpox vaccine. Those who received the vaccine got a scratch on the arm with a weakened version of the virus. The body reacted by becoming immune to the stronger smallpox virus.

Over the years, scientists perfected the vaccine, and the last case of smallpox reported in the world came from a man in Somalia in 1977. Smallpox has been essentially eradicated, though samples of the virus remain in at least two laboratories in the world. Americans have not been vaccinated against smallpox since 1972.

the test was made available, the risk of getting hepatitis from a blood transfusion is one in every 100,000 units transfused.

Hepatitis D, which depends on hepatitis B to survive, was discovered in 1978 by an Italian scientist named Mario Rizzetto. Hepatitis E was not discovered until 1983, when a Russian scientist named Mikhail Balayan noticed a new kind of hepatitis virus in localized epidemics, also spread by contaminated water. Today, scientists continue to learn about hepatitis. Some people get nonspecific viral liver disease after receiving blood transfusions. Doctors know little about this virus and sometimes refer to it as non A–non B hepatitis. Scientists are studying viral liver disease, trying to isolate it and then find a test to diagnose it. With increased research and universal vaccine against all types of hepatitis, it is possible that this disease, like smallpox, could be completely eradicated.

According to the Hepatitis B Foundation, every state except Alabama requires children to be immunized for hepatitis B. Depending on the state, the law requires children to be immunized by a certain age. For example, Colorado requires all children who attend day care to be immunized. In Iowa, children don't have to be immunized against hepatitis B until they are enrolled in elementary school.

Very few states require immunizations against hepatitis A, mostly because hepatitis A is so rare. Some states, such as Missouri and Montana, require food handlers to be vaccinated against the virus. Remember, it is easy to pass hepatitis A through food or water.

4

LIVING WITH HEPATITIS

For most people who get hepatitis A or B, it is an acute, or short-term, infection. People infected with hepatitis A or B get sick quickly. Their symptoms can be severe, but it is most often a one-time infection. With hepatitis C, and in some cases hepatitis B, the infection can be chronic. A chronic disease is one that makes a person sick for a long time. Most people diagnosed with hepatitis C will deal with the disease for their entire lives, and the virus could do serious damage to the liver over time.

Dealing with a disease can be both physically and emotionally difficult. Remember how relieved you feel when you get rid of your cold or get over the flu? People with a chronic disease can frequently feel sick, with little or no chance of a cure. Not only is that hard on the body, but it is also hard on the mind.

To make matters worse, the way in which someone contracted a disease can be embarrassing too. It's unfortunate to get hepatitis A from eating at a restaurant, but it's different to get a disease from sharing needles or having unprotected sex with someone who is infected. There can be a sense of shame or embarrassment from being infected. Even if someone got hepatitis C from a blood transfusion or because he or she was accidentally stuck with a diseased needle, the virus has a bad reputation. And since many people don't understand hepatitis, it is often the person with the disease who has to set them straight.

According to the book *Living with Hepatitis C*, only a minuscule amount of the virus is required to infect a human—the amount of blood it takes to cover the head of a pin is enough. Such a small amount of blood can get caught in the most random places, on razors or toothbrushes. Patients who are not regular intravenous drug users or who do not require frequent blood transfusions often have no idea how they acquired hepatitis C. Even one bad decision, like snorting cocaine at a party, can result in a hepatitis C infection. (Regular cocaine use often results in a hole developing between the nostrils. Sharing a straw to snort cocaine with someone who has this hole can lead to the transfer of diseased blood.) Even something common, such as getting a tattoo or a body piercing, can spread hepatitis if the tattoo or piercing gun is not properly sterilized.

Learning that a loved one has a disease can be difficult—especially if the friend or family member is unfamiliar with the disease. Can a man have unprotected sex with his wife if he has hepatitis C? Can they eat off the same plate and drink from the same glass? Can he hug and kiss his children without infecting them? Although the answer to all of these questions is yes, it can take a lot of time and patience to fully understand hepatitis C.

One way people with hepatitis C have to adjust is to change their diet. The liver is like the manager of the digestive system. It produces the bile that helps break down food and absorb fat. It stores energy and vitamins from food to send to other organs. Perhaps most important, the liver breaks down toxins in the body, including drugs and alcohol. People in the early stages of hepatitis C can maintain the same healthy diet as noninfected people. However, people with hepatitis C should not drink alcohol, as it causes more strain on their livers, can decrease the effectiveness of treatment, can increase the risk of cancer, and is also thought to increase the speed that the virus replicates.

Tattoo artist Jason Pierce works on a customer in April 2004 in Springfield, Illinois. The tattooing and piercing trend has caused some concern among those who track disease because of possible transmission through unsterile needles. Many states have increased their requirements for regulation and licensing of tattoo and piercing shops as a result.

People with advanced hepatitis C are sometimes put on a protein-restricted diet. They eat less meat and fish because their diseased livers cannot properly process protein. Too much protein in the system can cause encephalopathy, or clouding and confusion in the brain. Also, many people with hepatitis C feel less tired if they eat frequent, smaller meals instead of three big ones. It is easier for the liver to digest smaller amounts and spread energy throughout the day.

Treatment

The most common treatment of hepatitis C is called interferon therapy. Interferon is a natural substance that was discovered in 1957. Cells infected with a virus secrete a material that prevents other cells around it from being infected. Scientists called the material "interferon" because it "interfered" with the natural replication of the virus in the body. There are three classes, or types, of interferon: alpha, beta, and gamma. Only alpha interferon is used to treat hepatitis.

The pharmaceutical company Schering-Plough, Inc., created the first interferon therapy, a drug called Intron A. The U.S. Food and Drug Administration (FDA), the government agency that regulates drugs, approved Intron A for use for hepatitis in 1997. If effective, interferon therapy can prevent further damage to the liver. In some cases, interferon therapy suppresses the virus enough so it can no longer be detected in the blood. In some cases, the virus will gain strength after the patient stops taking the treatment.

In June 1998, the FDA approved another Schering-Plough drug, interferon alpha plus ribavirin, or Rebetron. Since December 1998, these combined drugs are the most commonly prescribed course of therapy for hepatitis C. Ribavirin is another drug that boosts the body's immune system. It fights hepatitis by helping interferons prevent the replication of the virus.

This is the crystal form of interferon, a drug that increases the activity of white blood cells. These types of drugs are very important in the fight against hepatitis, leukemia, and immunity-lowering diseases such as AIDS.

Interferon therapy involves injection of interferon. While many patients are concerned about giving themselves injections, interferon injections are subcutaneous. That means they are injected under the skin, which is not as painful as drugs that must be injected deep into muscles. Patients not only have to learn how to inject themselves but also how to store the drugs in their homes and how to safely dispose of needles.

Interferon therapy can also have side effects. The most common complaint among those using interferon therapy is they feel as though they have the flu. Since the body reacts to the flu by sending out interferon to fight the virus, it makes sense that elevated levels of interferon in the body can feel the same way. In a few cases, people feel depressed or lose their hair in reaction to interferon. Doctors monitor such side effects and often can control them by changing the dose of interferon a patient takes.

Besides trying to take care of themselves with medication and a healthful diet, people with hepatitis C may have to fight the depression that can accompany a chronic illness. Because hepatitis C can make a patient feel tired and sluggish, it makes it even harder to do other activities to take the mind off the disease. Also, because patients with hepatitis C are constantly monitoring their health with tests, sudden bad news can be emotionally troubling.

Several people with hepatitis C have been healthy their whole lives until the disease finally gets to them. People who love to ride bikes and go camping don't have the energy for it. Others who regularly stay out

Naomi Judd made her name famous as one-half of the mother-daughter country duo, the Judds. In a seven-year span, the Judds had twenty Top Ten songs, and Naomi won a Grammy Award for writing "Love Can Build a Bridge."

In 1991, the Judds stopped performing because Naomi had hepatitis C. Judd believes she got hepatitis C in the early 1980s, from a needle stick when she was working as an intensive-care unit nurse. Naomi went to a doctor because she was often tired, had a headache that wouldn't go away, and experienced some depression. As she told the University of Pittsburgh, "It was as if I could not see colors in their normal vibrancy."

In 1990, Naomi began interferon treatment, injecting the medicine into her abdomen. The interferon made her feel

Naomi and Wynonna Judd perform at the MGM Grand casino in Las Vegas, Nevada, in 2000. Naomi's fight against hepatitis has helped raise public awareness of the disease.

depressed and as if she had the flu, and doctors balanced the side effects with the antidepressant drug Zoloft. The medication worked for Naomi. Her body has been free of the hepatitis C virus since 1996.

Though she no longer has the virus, Naomi still spreads the word about hepatitis C. In 1991, she created the Naomi Judd Education and Research Fund to educate people about hepatitis. The fund also raises money for the American Liver Foundation. Naomi's fund started with $75,000 of her own money and has since raised more than $1 million. Naomi is also the spokesperson for the American Liver Foundation (ALF). The foundation's work goes toward the "prevention, treatment, and cure of hepatitis and other liver diseases," according to the ALF Web site.

late with friends need more sleep. Hepatitis forces the patient to change his or her lifestyle. No one likes having to curtail his or her activities. Also, feeling as though your body is turning against you is frustrating.

Beside medicine, people with hepatitis turn to other things to feel better. The Internet has linked hepatitis C patients to one another for the first time in history. Now patients can find others like them. People with hepatitis can compare treatments while online or share their stories with others who know exactly what they are going through. Sometimes knowing that there are other people experiencing the same symptoms can go a long way toward making someone feel better.

Conclusion

One of the most important things to remember about hepatitis is that scientists are still learning about the disease. Although humans have contracted hepatitis for thousands of years, it is only recently that scientists have identified it. Treatments for hepatitis are even more recent. Hepatitis C was not "discovered" until 1989, and treatments for it are still being developed. Doctors and scientists continue working on vaccines for hepatitis C. Vaccines successfully slowed the spread of hepatitis A and B, and a vaccine for hepatitis C could do the same.

Until scientists find a vaccine, there are new treatments for hepatitis C. One of the most promising is pegylated interferon therapy. In this medicine, polyethylene glycol (PEG) attaches itself to interferon. Pegylated interferon stays in the body longer than interferon alone. It works harder at helping the immune system fight hepatitis C. Also, some forms of pegylated interferon need only be injected once a week. Other hepatitis C drugs must be injected three times a week for six to twelve months.

Besides interferon therapy, scientists are examining other ways to treat hepatitis. Doctors are having some luck with interleukins. Interleukins are found naturally in the body and they fight infections. Some interleukins could help keep levels of hepatitis C down, or suppressed.

Protease inhibitors may also work against hepatitis C. A protease is a molecule found inside a virus that helps the virus reproduce. Protease inhibitors keep viruses from reproducing. Protease inhibitors are now used to treat HIV, though using them to fight hepatitis C is still in the early testing stages. However, one study showed that a single dose of protease inhibitor significantly reduced the amount of virus in the body only two days later.

It can take years between the time a scientist creates a drug that may help treat a disease and when a patient can pick up that drug at the pharmacy. Drugs must first go through several tests called clinical trials. These tests show the FDA whether a drug is safe and effective. In clinical trials, people volunteer to have a new drug tested on them. Some people volunteer for a clinical trial because no other medicine has worked on their illness. Others volunteer because they want to help doctors help others.

Many research studies are called blind studies. In a blind study, half the research volunteers will receive the new drug. The other half will take a placebo, or something that looks like the drug but actually has no effect on the body. The volunteers never know until the end of the study if they are

A Cornell University researcher inspects a tomato plant, part of an experiment to genetically engineer vaccines in food plants. Hepatitis B, cholera, lung infections, and sexually transmitted diseases are some of the diseases being targeted by this experiment.

taking the real drug or the placebo. By conducting a blind study, scientists can compare how the drugs work. Scientists call the research studies "blind" because patients do not know whether they are getting an actual drug or a placebo. (A "double blind" study means that doctors do not know which patients are getting an actual drug or a placebo.)

Clinical trials are conducted in three parts, or phases. In phase I, scientists test the drug on a small group of twenty to eighty people to figure out a safe dose and if there are any side effects. If a drug is found safe and useful in phase I, it can move along to other phases. Larger groups of volunteers are used in phases II and III. Finally, after the drug is approved and for sale to the public, a phase IV study will try to find any other side effects or new information about the drug.

In clinical trials, doctors have to follow specific rules, called a protocol. For phases II and III, so many volunteers are used that several doctors are needed to test the drug on all of them. A protocol makes sure all the volunteers in the clinical trial are treated the same way. Because new drugs can harm as well as heal, the FDA takes many precautions to make sure a drug is safe before making it available to the public.

Because clinical trials take so long, it could be years before a vaccine or medicine is found for hepatitis C. Until that time, it is crucial that people do their best to avoid the virus by not participating in risky behaviors. Like smallpox and polio, hepatitis is a disease that can be eliminated. Scientists will keep working to better help those who already have the disease and protect those who are free of the virus.

GLOSSARY

contaminate To expose something to disease.

contract To catch or acquire, as in a disease.

dehydration The excessive loss of water from the body.

diagnose To identify a disease or condition in a person.

eradicate To eliminate.

feces Human or animal solid waste.

hypothesis An idea that requires proof obtained from thorough research.

minuscule Very small or tiny.

organelle A structure within a cell that performs a specific function.

organ transplant The surgical replacement of a diseased organ with a healthy one.

precipice The brink of a dangerous or disastrous situation.

sterile Clean or free from bacteria.

stigma A mark of disgrace caused by bad behavior.

FOR MORE INFORMATION

In the United States

American Liver Foundation
75 Maiden Lane, Suite 603
New York, NY 10038
(212) 688-1000 or (800) 465-4837
e-mail: info@liverfoundation.org
Web site: http://www.liverfoundation.org

Centers for Disease Control and Prevention (CDC)
1600 Clifton Road
Atlanta, GA 30333
(404) 639-3534
(800) 311-3435
(800) 232-2522 (Immunization hotline)
Web site: http://www.cdc.gov

Hepatitis B Foundation
700 East Butler Avenue
Doylestown, PA 18901-2697
(215) 489-4900
e-mail: info@hepb.org
Web site: http://www.hepb.org

Hepatitis Foundation International
504 Black Drive
Silver Spring, MD 20904-2901
(301) 622-4200 or (800) 891-0707
e-mail: hfi@comcast.net
Web site: http://www.hepfi.org

Immunization Action Coalition
1573 Selby Avenue, Suite 234
St. Paul, MN 55104
(651) 647-9009
e-mail: admin@immunize.org
Web site: http://www.immunize.org

World Health Organization (WHO)
525 23rd Street NW
Washington, DC 20037
(202) 974-3000
Web site: http://www.who.int

In Canada

Canadian Digestive Health Foundation (CDHF)
CDHF National Office
2902 South Sheridan Way
Oakville, ON L6J7L6
(905) 829-3949 or (866) 819-2333
e-mail: CDHFoffice@CDHF.ca
Web site: http://www.cdhf.ca

Clinical Trials Research Center
IWK Grace Health Center
P.O. Box 3070
5850 University Avenue
Halifax, NS B3J 3G9
(902) 428-8141
Web site: http://www.dal.ca/~ctrc

Web Sites

Due to the changing nature of Internet links, the
Rosen Publishing Group, Inc., has developed an
online list of Web sites related to the subject of this
book. This site is updated regularly. Please use this
link to access the list:

http://www.rosenlinks.com/epid/hepa

FOR FURTHER READING

Blumberg, Baruch S. *Hepatitis B: The Hunt for a Killer Virus*. Princeton, NJ: The Princeton University Press, 2002.

Hayhurst, Chris. *Everything You Need to Know About Hepatitis C*. New York: The Rosen Publishing Group, Inc., 2003.

Sheen, Barbara. *Hepatitis* (Diseases and Disorders). New York: Lucent Books, 2002.

Weinberg, Hedy, Shira Shump, and Gregory T. Everson. *My Mom Has Hepatitis C*. Long Island City, NY: Hatherleigh Press, 2000.

BIBLIOGRAPHY

The American Liver Foundation. "Getting Hip to Hep-Liver Health Information." Retrieved March 26, 2004 (http://liverfoundation.org/db/articles/1026).

The American Liver Foundation. "Hepatitis B: Breaking the Cycle of Infection from Mother to Newborn." Retrieved March 26, 2004 (http://liverfoundation.org/db/articles/1036).

Centers for Disease Control and Prevention. "Viral Hepatitis." Retrieved March 25, 2004 (http://www.cdc.gov/ncidod/diseases/hepatitis).

Cuthbert, J. A. "Hepatitis A: Ancient Disease, Emerging Threat? A Modern Review With Historical Emphasis." *Clinical Microbiology Review*, 2001, pp. 38–58.

Epidemic.org. "Hepatitis C, an Epidemic for Anyone."
    Retrieved March 25, 2004 (http://www.
    epidemic.org/index2.html).
Everson, Gregory T., and Hedy Weinberg. *Living with
    Hepatitis C: A Survivor's Guide*. Long Island City,
    NY: Hatherleigh Press, 2002.
National Academy of Sciences Website. "The
    Hepatitis B Story." Retreived August 9, 2004
    (http://www.beyonddiscovery.org/content/
    view.article.asp?a=265).

INDEX

CREDITS

About the Author

Aileen Gallagher is a private investigator of financial firms and a freelance writer. She has written four previous books for the Rosen Publishing Group, Inc. Her freelance work has appeared in the *New York Law Journal* and the *National Law Journal*. She is an editor of BlackTable.com. She lives in New York City.

Photo Credits

Cover and chapter title interior photos © CDC/Dr. W. Winn; p. 4 © Sabrina Louise Pierce/AP/Wide World Photos; p. 6 © Gene J. Puskar/AP/Wide World Photos; p. 7 © David Maung/AP/Wide World Photos; p. 10 © Stephen Ferry/ Liaison/Getty Images; p. 14 © CDC/NCID; p. 16 © Michael Regan/AP/Wide World Photos; pp. 22, 36 © Time Life Pictures/Getty Images; p. 27 © CDC/ Public Health Image Library/PHIL/Dr. Thomas F. Sellers/Emory University; p. 32 courtesy of Dr. Harvey Alter; p. 37 © CDC/Public Health Image Library/PHIL/James Gathany; p. 38 © NLM/J. Ryst; p. 44 © Seth Perlman/AP/Wide World Photos; p. 46 © James King-Holmes/Photo Researchers, Inc.; p. 48 © Scott Harrison/Hulton Archive/Getty Images; p. 52 © Michael J. Okoniewski/Getty Images.

Designer: Evelyn Horovicz; Editor: Joann Jovinelly;
Photo Researcher: Hillary Arnold